Sam Cat and Nat Rat

Written and Illustrated
by Shelley Davidow

Jalmar Press

ISBN: 978-1-931061-44-5

Jalmar Press
PO Box 370
Fawnskin, CA 92333
(800) 429-1192
F: (909) 866-2961
www.jalmarpress.com

About the Author and Illustrator: Shelley Davidow is originally from South Africa. Her young adult book, *In the Shadow of Inyangani*, was nominated for the first African Writer's Prize by Macmillan/Picador and BBC World. The author of numerous books, Shelley lives in Florida (USA), where she is a class teacher at the Sarasota Waldorf School.

About the Readers: These early readers are phonetically based and contain stories that young children will find enjoyable and entertaining. Each story has a beginning, middle and an ending. The stories are gently humorous while honoring nature, animals and the environment.

The six books use simple words that the early reader will easily grasp. They have been carefully chosen by a reading specialist to help students advance from the short vowels, to the silent "e", to the vowel combinations. At the back of this book is a list of sight words that should be reviewed with the child before reading the book.

About our Reading Specialist: Mary Spotts has been a remedial reading teacher for over ten years, taking countless classes and seminars to keep current in the field she loves. Her deep under-standing that struggling readers need good stories — particularly if the books are phonetically based — has been an inspiration in the creation of these books. Mary has been a constant guide, ensuring that the books address specific phonetic principles while retaining a gently humorous story line.

Mary's desire to have available meaningful children's stories with decodable words and Shelley's creative talents and love of literature have been the incentive and encouragement to bring these books to production.

For Sadie

Sam Cat sat on his soft mat.
Sam Cat sat and sat.

Sam Cat did not get up.
He sat. Then he slept.

Nat Rat ran.

Nat Rat ran and ran.

Nat Rat ran up to Sam Cat.

Nat Rat crept up
onto Sam Cat.

Sam Cat and Nat Rat

Sam Cat was soft.

Sam Cat was soft and fat.

He just slept and slept.

Nat Rat sat on top of
Sam Cat and had a rest.

A rat sat on a cat!

Sam Cat got up.

Nat Rat went up and up and up!

Sam Cat and Nat Rat

Then Sam Cat saw Nat Rat.

Nat Rat ran.

Sam Cat ran.

Stop, rat! Stop!

Sam Cat went to get Nat Rat.

Stop, cat! Stop!

Nat Rat went up to Sam Cat.

Sam Cat and Nat Rat
went to sit on the mat.

Sam and Nat, a cat and
a rat, sat on a soft mat.

Sam Cat and Nat Rat

Short Vowel Sounds

a	e	i	o	u
cat	get	did	got	up
fat	then	sit	not	just
mat	went	his	top	
sat	rest		stop	
rat	slept		on	
Nat	crept		soft	
ran				
Sam				
had				
and				

Sight Words

he

to

was

of

a

saw

the

onto

CPSIA information can be obtained at www.ICGtesting.com
Printed in the USA
BVOW02s2233260615

406064BV00001B/2/P

9 781931 061445